The Beauty
of Bali

Written by Sharon Fear

Celebration Press

Parsippany, New Jersey

INDONESIA

Bali

INDIAN

OCEAN

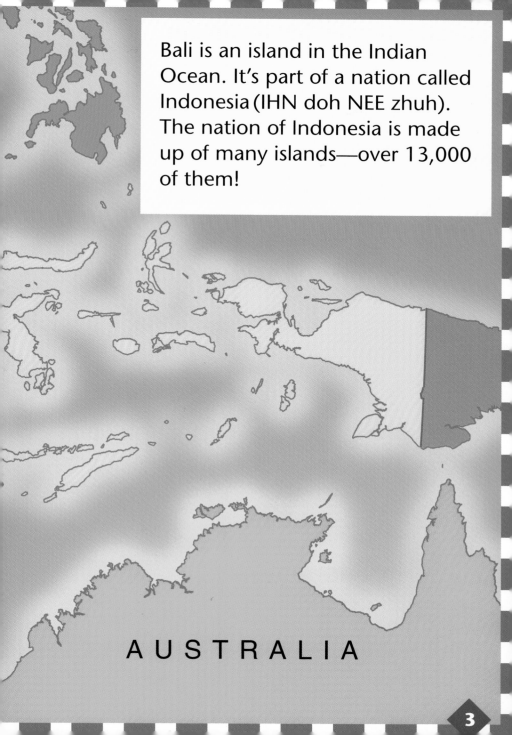

Bali is an island in the Indian Ocean. It's part of a nation called Indonesia (IHN doh NEE zhuh). The nation of Indonesia is made up of many islands—over 13,000 of them!

AUSTRALIA

It is usually warm and wet in Bali. Palm trees and bamboo grow there. Monkeys and tropical birds live in Bali's forests.

Bali has many mountains. Some of them used to be active volcanoes. Mount Agung, the highest point in Bali, is still an active volcano. It last erupted in 1963.

Lava from these volcanoes has made rich soil that is good for growing crops. People in Bali grow fruit, vegetables, and coffee, but Bali's main crop is rice. Farmers build flat gardens on the steep hills. They dig ditches to carry water from rivers to the rice paddies.

Rice needs a lot of water to grow. Because there is so much water, rice paddies can also be homes to animals, such as ducks and eels. Bali is famous for these beautiful rice paddies.

Bali is also famous for its music, its dance, and its shadow puppets. People from all over the world visit Bali to see these amazing performances.

Almost every village in Bali has a gamelan (GAM uh lahn). This is a group of people who play special kinds of gongs and drums.

The gamelan always plays for dances. Some of these dances are a thousand years old. They tell stories of Bali's past and tales of Balinese heroes.

Bali's most famous dance is the legong (LUH gong). Young girls do this dance. They begin to learn the dance when they are five years old.

Men dance wearing masks. These dances tell ancient stories. Each mask stands for a different story character.

Some of the same stories are told with shadow puppets. The puppets are flat and made of leather or wood.

One person, the dalang (DAH lang), puts on the whole play. He uses an oil lamp to throw the puppets' shadows onto a cloth screen. He moves the puppets. He tells the story. He makes the sounds. He tells the gamelan when to play. These shadow plays often last all night. Everyone knows the stories. They have been told for hundreds of years.

People watch and listen closely, for these plays are an important part of Bali's past—and of Bali's present.